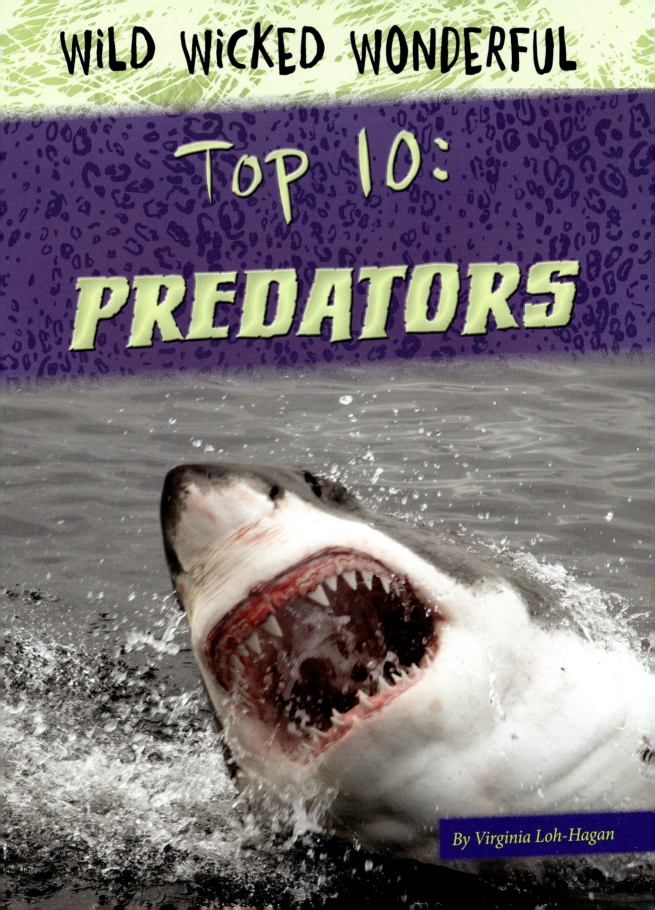

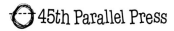
## 45th Parallel Press

Published in the United States of America by Cherry Lake Publishing
Ann Arbor, Michigan
www.cherrylakepublishing.com

Content Adviser: Stephen Ditchkoff, Professor of Wildlife Ecology and Management, Auburn University, Alabama
Reading Adviser: Marla Conn, ReadAbility, Inc.
Book Designer: Melinda Millward

Photo Credits: ©Pieter De Pauw/iStockphoto, cover, 1, 23; ©J Parker/Shutterstock Images, 5; ©Audrey Snider-Bell/Shutterstock Images, 6, 16; ©Enrique Ramos/Shutterstock Images, 6; ©Netfalls - Remy Musser/Shutterstock Images, 6; ©Trevor kelly/Shutterstock Images, 7; ©Johan Swanepoel/Shutterstock Images, 8; © Nawaj Panichphol/Dreamstime.com, 10; © Stephen Dalton/Minden Pictures/Corbis, 11; © Anthony Hathaway/Dreamstime.com, 12; ©Sylvie Bouchard/Shutterstock Images, 12; ©EstelleHood/Thinkstock, 12; ©pum_eva/Thinkstock, 13; ©papkin/Shutterstock Images, 14; ©SonNumber4/Thinkstock, 14; ©Kucher Serhii/Shutterstock Images, 14; ©Cathy Keifer/Shutterstock Images, 15; ©reptiles4all/Shutterstock Images, 16; ©Sprocky/Shutterstock Images, 16; © Igor Pershin/Dreamstime.com, 17; ©Maria Dryfhout/Shutterstock Images, 18; ©ewastudio/Thinkstock, 19; © Yourthstock/Dreamstime.com, 20; ©Stacey Newman/Shutterstock Images, 20; ©Clay_Harrison/Thinkstock, 20; © WaterFrame / Alamy Stock Photo, 21; ©Sergey Uryadnikov/Shutterstock Images, 22; ©Jim Agronick/Shutterstock Images, 22; ©Elsa Hoffmann/Shutterstock Images, 22; ©vladoskan/Thinkstock, 24; ©Bildagentur Zoonar GmbH/Shutterstock Images, 26; ©Tom Tietz/Shutterstock Images, 26; ©Erni/Shutterstock Images, 26, 30; ©kochanowski/Shutterstock Images, 27; © Kstokvis/Dreamstime.com, 28; ©Karoline Cullen/Shutterstock Images, 28; ©Stephen Lew/Shutterstock Images, 29; © blickwinkel / Alamy Stock Photo, 31

Graphic Element Credits: © tukkki/Shutterstock Images, back cover, front cover, multiple interior pages; © paprika/Shutterstock Images, back cover, front cover, multiple interior pages; © Silhouette Lover/Shutterstock Images, multiple interior pages

Copyright © 2016 by Cherry Lake Publishing

All rights reserved. No part of this book may be reproduced or utilized in any form or by any means without written permission from the publisher.

**45th Parallel Press** is an imprint of Cherry Lake Publishing.

Library of Congress Cataloging-in-Publication Data

Loh-Hagan, Virginia, author.
　Top 10 : predators / by Virginia Loh-Hagan.
pages cm. — (Wild wicked wonderful)
ISBN 978-1-63470-505-9 (hardcover) — ISBN 978-1-63470-625-4 (pbk.) — ISBN 978-1-63470-565-3 (pdf) — ISBN 978-1-63470-685-8 (ebook)
1. Predatory animals—Juvenile literature. 2. Predation (Biology)—Juvenile literature. I. Title. II. Title: Predators. III. Title: Top ten : predators.
QL758.L64 2016
591.5'3—dc23　　　　　　　　2015026857

Printed in the United States of America
Corporate Graphics

## About the Author

Dr. Virginia Loh-Hagan is an author, university professor, former classroom teacher, and curriculum designer. She's a piano-predator. She has three pianos. She just hunted down a 7-foot Steinway. She lives in San Diego with her very tall husband and very naughty dogs. To learn more about her, visit www.virginialoh.com.

# TABLE OF CONTENTS

Introduction ............................................................................. 4

Chapter one
Crocodiles ............................................................................. 6

Chapter two
Archerfish ............................................................................ 10

Chapter three
Polar Bears ......................................................................... 12

Chapter four
Spiders ................................................................................ 14

Chapter five
Snakes ................................................................................ 16

Chapter six
Electric Eels ........................................................................ 20

Chapter seven
Great White Sharks ........................................................... 22

Chapter eight
Wolves ................................................................................ 26

Chapter nine
Orcas ................................................................................... 28

Chapter ten
Shrews ................................................................................ 30

Consider This! ..................................................................... 32
Glossary .............................................................................. 32
Index .................................................................................... 32

# INTRODUCTION

Animals hunt. They're **predators**. Predators are hunters. They **lure**. They draw **prey** in. Prey are animals that are hunted for food. Predators **stalk** prey. They follow them. They trick them. Then they attack. They harm. They kill.

Predators hunt to eat. They eat to **survive**. Survive means to stay alive. They need food to live. They have different ways of hunting.

All animals are part of a food chain. Animals can be prey for some animals. They can also be predators to other animals.

Some animals are extreme predators. Their hunts are bigger. Their hunts are better. They're the most exciting predators in the animal world!

*Predators are part of life. All living things need to eat.*

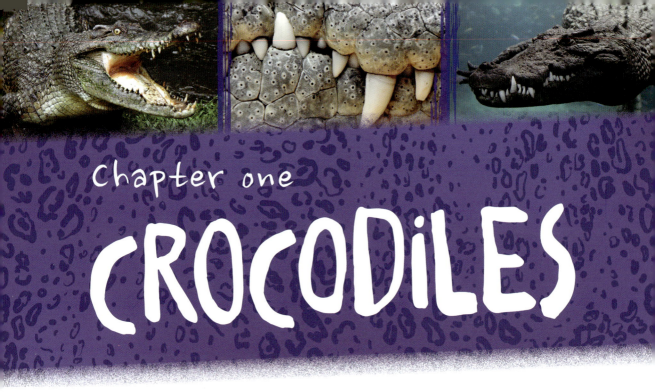

# Chapter one
# CROCODILES

Crocodiles are three times longer than male humans. And they're 10 times heavier. Saltwater crocodiles are the largest land predators. They kill about 2,000 humans a year.

Their brains are the size of a human thumb. But they're smart hunters. Crocodiles can hold their breath. They can do it for about an hour. They hide in the water. They wait. They watch. They might wait for a month before they eat. They study their killing grounds.

Their eyes and nose are just above the water. They look like floating logs. They trick prey. They wait for prey to come.

*Crocodiles can crush their prey in their jaws.*

Then, they **ambush**. They attack without warning. They just need one big meal. This gives them enough energy for a year.

*Crocodiles eat anything that floats into their mouths.*

Crocodiles have the strongest bite. Their bite is 10 times stronger than humans'. They have powerful jaws. Their jaws have many muscles. They slam shut.

Crocodiles have 60 to 80 teeth. They replace their teeth. They do it about 50 times before they die. Their teeth are shaped like cones. They're sharp. But they can't tear flesh. So they grab their prey. They hold them. They drive their teeth into them. Prey can't escape. They're locked in. They're trapped.

Crocodiles look slow. But they strike fast. They have special stomachs. Their stomachs can break down bones, hooves, and horns. They can eat anything.

# Humans Do What?!?

Some humans hunt big game. Big game refers to big animals. These hunters hunt animals like lions, elephants, and rhinos. They mainly hunt in Africa. They pay a lot of money. They take home animal heads, skins, or horns. But many think hunting big game for sport is wrong. In 2015, a group of hunters killed Cecil the Lion. Cecil lived in the Hwange National Park in Zimbabwe. The hunters led Cecil out of the park. They wounded Cecil with an arrow. They followed Cecil for 40 hours. They shot Cecil with a gun. Then they removed Cecil's skin and head as a trophy. One of the hunters paid $50,00 to kill Cecil. Cecil was a special lion. He was popular. His mane had a black fringe. A university was studying him. Cecil was killed for no reason. Many people used social media to make big game hunters feel bad about their actions. Some humans hurt animals. But, many humans want to protect them.

# chapter two
# ARCHERFISH

Archerfish live in special forests. These forests grow in water. Archerfish live under the trees. They swim among tree roots. They live in Southeast Asia.

They look above the water. They look for bugs on leaves. They have super eyesight. They're **archers**. They're hunters who aim and shoot. They shoot water. They have special mouthparts. They can shoot bugs about 6 feet (1.8 meters) above the water.

They search for bugs. They spit at their prey. They spit at an angle. They spit a jet of water. Their spit is 16 feet (4.9 m)

*Young archerfish learn by hunting in small groups, or schools.*

long. They do this in less than a second. They knock prey into the water. They rarely miss. If they do, they keep trying. Then they eat!

## Chapter three
# POLAR BEARS

Polar bears live in the Arctic. They live on the frozen **ice pack**. The ice pack is hard layers of ice over the ocean. Finding prey is hard. Not many living things can live in the Arctic. It's too cold.

Adult polar bears weigh as much as seven men. They attack prey three times their size. They attack with one swipe of their paws.

They hunt with their noses. They have a super sense of smell. They smell 100 times better than humans can. They can smell out seals. They smell seals 20 miles (32 kilometers)

*Polar bears are successful in about 10 percent of their attacks on seals under the ice.*

away. They smell seals under 3 feet (91 centimeters) of ice. They use their big paws. They break the ice. They devour prey.

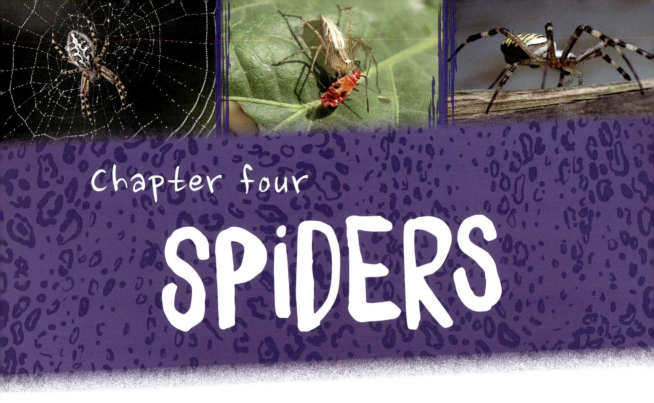

## Chapter four
# SPIDERS

There are more than 35,000 different kinds of spiders. They're all predators. They hunt bugs.

They trap their prey. They have silk. They make webs. Their webs are strong. They're flexible. They can hold 4,000 times their weight. Prey fly into spider webs. They get stuck. Then spiders wrap them up. They eat them.

Some spiders go fishing. They release a single thread. The thread goes into the wind. It catches a bug. Spiders pull up the thread. They attach the thread to their web.

*Spiders use their webs like weapons.*

Some spiders have moving webs. They aim at prey. They throw out webs. Their webs are like nets.

## Chapter five
# SNAKES

Snakes are great hunters. They track down prey. They hunt at night. They hunt during the day.

They have very strong senses. They smell the air. They use their tongues. They have super eyesight. They see small movements.

Some have pits on the sides of their faces. These pits see special light. Humans can't see this light. They can only feel its heat. These pits send information to the brain. Snakes see the heat of their prey.

*Snakes can get into all kinds of spaces. This makes it easier for them to hunt.*

This means nothing can hide. Snakes can see and feel prey. Snakes don't kill often. It takes them awhile to swallow and **digest**. Digest is how bodies break down food.

*Snakes have four rows of teeth on the top. They have two rows on the bottom.*

Most snakes have teeth. Snakes use teeth to hunt prey. Some snakes' teeth are like needles. They're called **fangs**. Fangs are long, sharp teeth. They put holes in skin. They dig deep. They inject poison.

Snakes fold their fangs into their mouths. They don't want to bite themselves. Their fangs come out when they strike.

Snakes have a strong bite **reflex**. It's an instant movement. They just bite once. They bite quickly. Then they move away. Their bite takes less than a second.

Snakes still bite after they die. Even if snakes get chopped in two. Snake heads will keep biting. Their nerves still work.

# When Animals Attack!

"Mysterious Queen" is the name of a man-eating tiger. It's a Bengal tigress. It lives in northern India. It has killed at least 10 people. Its first victim was a young farmer before his wedding day. Some people believe the tiger escaped from a zoo. They think she lost her cubs and is seeking revenge. A tiger expert said, "When a tiger turns into a man-eater, it becomes faster and shrewder. ... It uses an uncanny sense of sight and touch to move toward people." Another expert said, "Once they become man-eaters, they become invisible, very cunning, just like ghosts." This means the tiger is quick and smart. It hasn't been seen. It hunts over about 150 square miles (388 square km). It hunts through villages, fields, and forests. It crosses rivers. It crosses highways. Hunters can't catch the tiger. They tried setting traps. They tried luring it with bait. They can't find it.

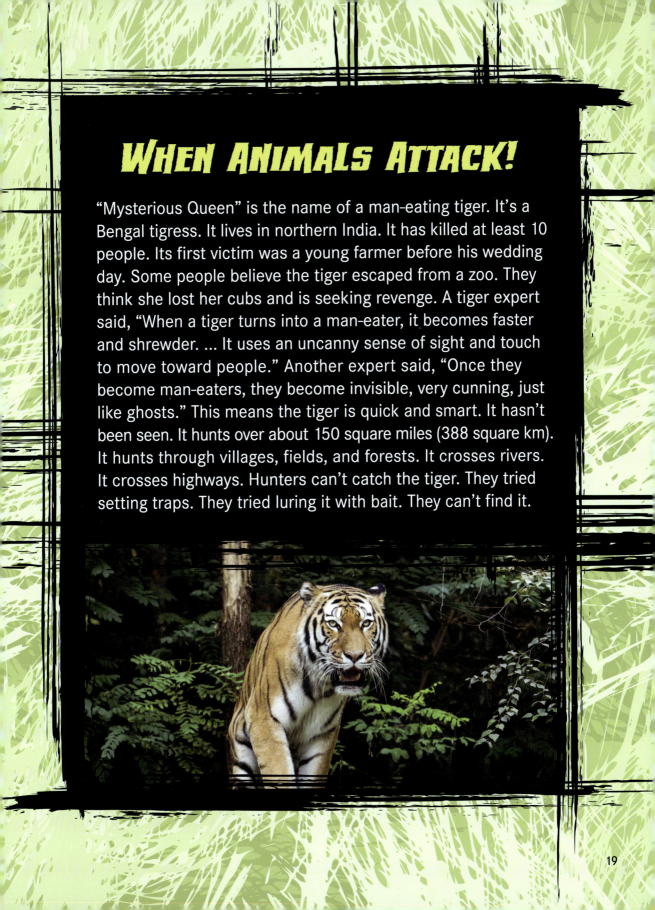

## Chapter Six
# ELECTRIC EELS

Electric eels live in the Amazon river. They aren't really eels. They're more like catfish. They're huge. They're about 6 feet (1.8 m) long. They weigh 44 pounds (20 kilograms). They surface to breathe. They can't see well. But they have power.

Their tails have **voltage**. Voltage is electricity. Electric eels have about 6,000 cells. These cells store power. They're like tiny batteries.

They use low-voltage pulses. This is how they **navigate**. They find their way. They find fish. They hunt.

Electric eels shock their prey with electricity.

They use high voltage. They zap their prey. All their cells work at the same time. They release 600 volts. That's five times more powerful than a power socket. They stun their prey.

## Chapter seven
# GREAT WHITE SHARKS

Great white sharks are the largest predatory fish. They grow to 20 feet (6 m) long. They weigh 4,000 pounds (1,814 kg). They have 2 tons of muscles.

They are named for their white bellies. But they are dark on top. They blend into the water. They attack from below. They change direction. They ambush their prey.

They are great hunters. But they work hard to find prey. They have special organs. They have super eyesight. They have super hearing. They have super smelling ability. Tiny

*Great white sharks sneak up on their prey.*

holes are around their snout. They sense electricity as animals move. They feel movements. They're fast.

*Great white sharks use gills to breathe. Their skin has little tooth-like scales or denticles.*

Great white sharks have strong jaws. They have 200 sharp teeth in five rows. Their teeth can get stuck in prey. They lose and replace teeth.

They can go for weeks without killing. They eat injured and sick animals. They also eat dead whale bodies. They are helpful. They keep the oceans' wildlife balanced.

Great white sharks are scary. But they're scarier in our minds. Falling coconuts kill more people than great white sharks. Humans taste bad to them.

#  Did You Know…?

- Electric eels aren't the only ones that use electricity. Police officers use tasers. Tasers are electric shock devices. They deliver 50,000 volts of electricity. They stun criminals.

- Hunters have copied wolves' hunting style. Native Americans saw wolves as teachers. They copied the way wolves work together.

- Today, many Americans are obese. Part of the problem is that humans are no longer predators. Hunting burns body fat. Now, we get food from grocery stores.

- Crocodiles sit in the sun all day. They use the same amount of energy as a sparrow.

- Shocks from electric eels affect people. They cause breathing problems. They cause heart failure. Some people have drowned after being stunned. But human deaths from the eels are rare.

- To keep up with shrews, humans would have to eat 1,920 hamburgers each day.

- Wolves have two layers of fur. They have a top coat and an undercoat. This allows them to live in cold temperatures. When it's warm, they flatten their fur.

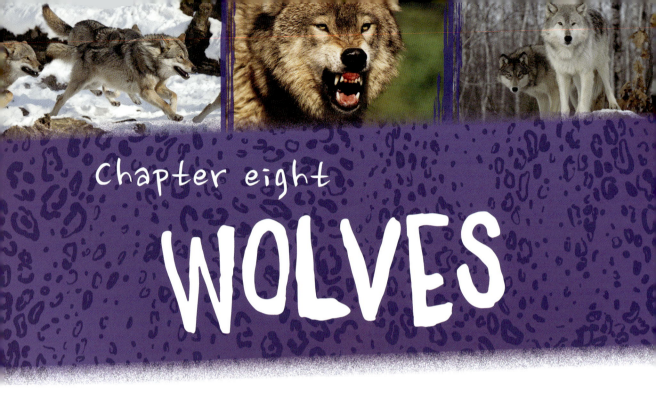

## Chapter eight
# WOLVES

Wolves eat anything to survive. They eat animals eight times bigger. They hunt large deer, moose, or elk. They hunt as a pack. They pick prey. They run it down. They attack from all sides. They rip away legs. They rip at the guts. They wait for prey to fall down. Then they eat right away. They eat prey while it is still alive.

In some places, wolves are needed for balance. Lots of moose cause problems. Wolves are needed to eat some. They eat moose in their area. They eat almost 50 moose each year. Lots of wolves cause problems too. They eat too much! There needs to be balance.

Only one out of 10 wolf attacks is successful. Wolves kill at least once a week.

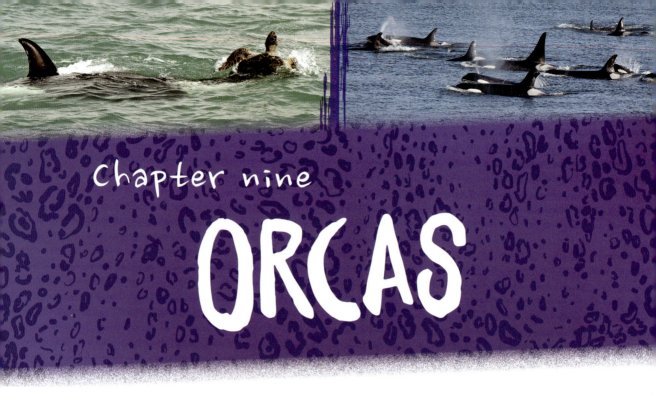

# Chapter nine
# ORCAS

Orcas are killer whales. They have the biggest brains of all whales. They're as big as elephants. They swim six times faster than Olympic swimmers.

They're called the "wolves of the sea." A group of orcas is a **pod**. A pod works together. They hunt like a wolf pack. They ambush their prey. They attack at high speeds. They ram into their prey. They throw preys' bodies out of the water. They break spines. They cause injuries.

They also chase prey. They chase for hours. Their prey gets tired. They give up. Orcas can kill anything in the sea.

*Orcas like to eat tongues and soft flesh.*

They even kill great white sharks!

They're not natural-born predators. They learn to kill from their mothers.

29

## chapter ten
# SHREWS

Shrews are small. But they're scary. Shrews have to eat all the time. They move all the time. Their hearts beat 600 times a minute. They have to eat at least their own body weight every day.

Shrews kill every two hours. Or they'll die. No other animal has to kill so often. They're good hunters. They have super smelling ability. Their whiskers help them find prey.

They attack prey 20 times their size. Their spit is poisonous. They **paralyze** their prey. They make it so their prey can't

*Shrews are the smallest mammal. But they eat a lot!*

move. They keep their prey alive. This is so they can eat for a long time. They graze on their prey for several days.

## CONSIDER THIS!

**TAKE A POSITION!** Predators get a bad reputation. But they need to eat. Do you think killing is a necessary part of life? Argue your point with reasons and evidence.

**SAY WHAT?** Explain how animals can be both predators and prey.

**THINK ABOUT IT!** Humans aren't used to being prey. But humans are taking over more animal habitats. This puts them in more contact with predators like tigers. Most animals do not attack humans without reason. Who's to blame for animal attacks?

**LEARN MORE!**
- Burnie, David. *Predator*. New York: DK Publishing, 2011.
- Townsend, John. *Amazing Predators*. Chicago: Raintree, 2013.

## GLOSSARY

**ambush (AM-bush)** to attack by surprise or without warning

**archers (AHRCH-urz)** hunters who aim and shoot

**digest (dye-JEST)** to break down food

**fangs (FANGZ)** long, sharp teeth

**ice pack (AYSE pak)** hard layers of ice over the ocean

**lure (LOOR)** to draw victims in

**navigate (NAV-ih-gate)** to find a way

**paralyze (PAR-uh-lize)** to make it so animals can't move

**pod (PAHD)** a group of orcas

**predators (PRED-uh-turz)** hunters

**prey (PRAY)** animals that are hunted for food

**reflex (REE-fleks)** an instant movement

**stalk (STAWK)** to follow

**survive (sur-VIVE)** to stay alive

**voltage (VOHL-tij)** electricity

## INDEX

archerfish, 10–11
bite, 8, 18
crocodiles, 6–8, 25
electric eels, 20–21, 25
electricity, 20–21, 23, 25
eyesight, 10, 16, 19, 22
great white sharks, 22–24
hearing, 22
heat, 16
humans, 6, 9, 24–25
jaws, 8, 24
orcas, 28–29
poison, 30–31
polar bears, 12–13
shrews, 25, 30–31
smell, sense of, 12–13, 16, 22, 30
snakes, 16–18
spiders, 14–15
spit, 10–11, 30–31
teeth, 8, 18, 24
voltage, 20–21
webs, 14–15
wolves, 25, 26–27, 28